26 STEPS

Controlled Composition for Intermediate and Advanced Language Development

Second Revised Edition

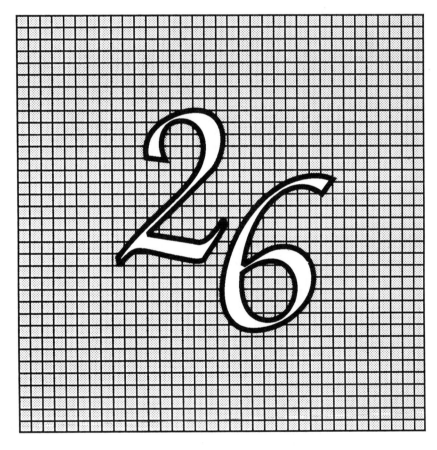

Linda Ann Kunz

Alemany Press

Prentice Hall Regents, Englewood Cliffs, NJ 07632

Companion Text

10 Steps

Controlled Composition for Beginning and Intermediate Language Development

by Gay Brookes and Jean Withrow

Student Book © 1988 (Second Revised Edition). 72 pp.
Teacher's Manual © 1988 (Second Revised Edition). 12 pp.
Published by Prentice Hall, Inc.

Project Editor: John Duffy
Copy Editor: Deborah Kransberg
Production/Design/Cover: E. Carol Gee
Composition: Arlene Hardwick, Elizabeth Tong

 © 1988 by Prentice-Hall, Inc.
A Simon & Schuster Company
Englewood Cliffs, New Jersey 07632

Printed in the United States of America

10 9 8 7 6 5 4

ISBN 0-13-933722-9

Prentice-Hall International (UK) Limited, *London*
Prentice-Hall of Australia Pty. Limited, *Sydney*
Prentice-Hall Canada Inc., *Toronto*
Prentice-Hall Hispanoamericana, S.A., *Mexico*
Prentice-Hall of India Private Limited, *New Delhi*
Prentice-Hall of Japan, Inc., *Tokyo*
Simon & Schuster Asia Pte. Ltd., *Singapore*
Editora Prentice-Hall do Brasil, Ltda., *Rio de Janeiro*

Contents

Preface to the Second Revised Edition

Dear Teacher and Student,

26 Steps is both the same as, and different from, its first edition published in 1973. As its author, I am the same and different, too, and the changes in us are deeply related.

I am grateful to the people who made possible the first edition: Christina Bratt Paulston and Gerald Dykstra, from whom I learned controlled composition at Teachers College, Columbia University; Robert R. Viscount, my co-author of *Write Me a Ream*, a controlled composition text for adult job training published by Teachers College Press; and the members of Language Innovations, Inc. (LINC), who wrote several of the early passages and published the first edition on a not-for-profit basis. Those people believed, as I do, that students can learn from and enjoy writing practice that takes the *form* of whole compositions while concentrating essentially on one feature of English grammar, sentence structure, or vocabulary at a time.

Also in 1973, I began to study the philosophy which would revolutionize my life and teaching, the Aesthetic Realism of Eli Siegel. Mr. Siegel was the first person to state this principle:

The purpose of education is to like the world through knowing it.

The way to like the world, he explained, is to see how it is made, how it is a oneness of opposites making for beauty, as shown in art as well as in every subject studied in school. Aesthetic Realism is taught at the Aesthetic Realism Foundation, a not-for-profit educational foundation based in New York City.

Studying Aesthetic Realism has explained and affirmed the best things I was doing in my teaching and writing and changed the things I could not be proud of. In *26 Steps*, for example, I see a relation of sameness and change that is reassuring yet challenging to students: there is so much of a passage that is already complete and correct together with a closely related group of changes. And the relatedness of these changes shows some of the logic and beauty of English. English, like all languages, shows the structure of the world in how it puts together opposites: vowels and consonants, masculine and feminine, singular and plural, past and present tenses, direct and indirect speech, active and passive voice, negative and affirmative statements, pre- and post-modifiers, dependent and independent clauses. It is these opposites that students work on as they move from step to step in the book.

Through my study of Aesthetic Realism, I am questioning and changing the way I see the world, and one result is the changing content of *26 Steps*. Nearly half of the original passages have been replaced altogether, and many others have been altered on behalf of greater fairness to, and accuracy about, people and things in the world. I am proud of passages added in 1979 and 1987, like "Old Is Beautiful," "A Good Friend," and one based on a student composition, "Fire and I"; at the same time I am questioning old standbys like "Cancerians" and "Capricornians," which work well grammatically but are simply untrue. I would like further changes in *26 Steps*, as well as other grammar books I plan to write, to be accurate in form *and* content because people learning English and working to improve their English deserve both.

So while *26 Steps* cannot be called an Aesthetic Realism textbook, it is one at its best influenced by Aesthetic Realism. I look forward to a time in the near future when teachers know this kind and true philosophy and when their textbooks reflect it; when a grammar class might begin: "As we study active and passive voice, class, we'll try to see how other things in the world are active and passive, too, and how *we* are...and the purpose of this class is to like the whole world more."

Linda Ann Kunz
New York City

Introduction

What Controlled Composition Is and Is Not

Controlled Composition is the use of **model passages** with accompanying instructions (or **steps**) to provide sequential, highly structured practice of grammar points, proofreading, sentence combining and vocabulary building without a lot of technical terminology. It is *not* free composition. It will not help students to develop and organize their ideas, to gather information or to illustrate a point. But it will make them think about what they put on a sheet of paper. It will make them pay attention to details. Most important, it will give them a *sheaf* of good-looking, 90-100% correct, full-size compositions that they can be proud of. And much as teachers preach the virtues of mistakes and what we can learn from them, students love perfection. Controlled composition gives them periodic perfection, which they strive for and earn.

From a teacher's point of view, controlled composition is individualized, high-volume backup writing; it is fast to get into and mark, and students like it, so they progress swiftly and can see their progress because the steps are numbered. These features have made controlled composition popular around the world for more than 30 years.

Who *26 Steps* Is For

26 Steps is a collection of 48 model passages designed for high school, college and adult bilingual students with basic English fluency and at least a little writing proficiency. Real beginners should use the companion volume *10 Steps* (second revised edition) by Gay Brookes and Jean Withrow.

How to Use this Text

If a whole class is to begin using *26 Steps* together, the best way to start is with the **Demonstration Passage** on page 1. Here is an introductory lesson.

1. Copy the Demonstration Passage on the board making a few errors in spelling, capitalization, etc. Have students **proofread** the composition— that is, read it very carefully in search of errors. Underline each error found.

2. When all errors have been found, ask students to copy the passage from their books or from the board *with the corrections but with none of the superscript sentence numbers*. Ask them if they think it is easy to make errors just copying and how copying and proofreading might be useful to people. Explain that a perfect copy enables a person to move to the next step, a step 2. Then check everyone's composition swiftly by walking around the class writing either "OK— Go on to step 2" or the number of errors you see.

3. Either have students follow the other steps beneath the Demonstration Passage in writing or have different students do those steps on the board. In either case the objectives are (a) to get across the ideas of **model passage, steps** and **proofreading**, (b) to have students *experience* the effect of English grammatical ties causing many changes from one change, and (c) to accustom them to a fast way of getting feedback and moving on.

4. When students seem comfortable with the procedures, have them find the model passage called "The Light-Fingered Elephant" alphabetically. (It happens that this passage is right in the middle of the book, and you will be able to tell whether some students are not accustomed to finding things this way.) Be sure students understand that they are to copy everything from the title to the last word but *not* the sentence numbers or step instructions. Also, they should

ignore the other step (step 3) on that passage and *always do only one step at a time*. They should also, from the outset, get into the fine habits of using looseleaf (instead of notebook) paper, writing their complete name and date and the step they're working on in the upper right corner and skipping lines. When they finish, they should record their work on the **Student Record Sheet** on page 55.

5. As students finish, mark their compositions as you did with the Demonstration Passage. The only difference is that now students may move *horizontally* as well as vertically, and they will go on to a different model passage. Use the **Sequence of Passages on Each Step** on pages 57-8 to determine what passage to prescribe next. For example, if a student has made three errors copying "The Light-Fingered Elephant", the top of her paper should look like this:

3 errors	Do another Step 1, "Coffee Breakthrough" Students' Complete Name June 18, 1990 Step 1
	the Light-fingered elephant
₱	Petal, the Philadelphia Zoo's 15-years-old African elephant, thought zookeeper
	Ed Recotta had some candy in his pocket. Many zookeepers do carry candy,

A Few Usage Notes

Most teachers have their own marking symbols, but it is essential *not to correct errors*. Many students will stand over a teacher's shoulder as he corrects and spot things a split second before an error is marked. The proofing gets passionate, and this seems to be a good thing. Still, just the marking of an error— even one— makes for a horizontal, rather than a vertical move, and your use of the Sequence of Passages, arranged so that students seldom reuse a passage, is crucial. And it *is* for your use only. Ask students not to do a second composition before you have marked the first. The Sequence of Passages is also useful in telling you if a student seems stuck on a particular step and needs extra help.

Sometimes students who are moving along nicely are staggered when they first try step 4 because of the sheer number of changes needed to go from plural to singular. It's kind to warn them that steps 4 and 5 usually need 30 or more changes per composition simply because English makes a very big deal of singular and plural (not as much as Spanish but so very much more than Chinese!).

26 Steps can be used in a lab, and some teachers have prepared answer sheets (which don't exist commercially), including an answer key on tape. The nature of the passages has also led to their use as culture and lifestyle readings. Rumor has it that some of the passages provoke heated discussion and lively free writing. Experiment and enjoy!

Demonstration Passage

In the Street

¹There is a policeman in the street.   ²He is stopping traffic.   ³There is a car at the corner.   ⁴A woman is inside it   ⁵There is a boy on the sidewalk.   ⁶He is riding his bicycle.   ⁷The bicycle is a two-wheeler.

Steps

1.   Copy the entire passage.

2.   Rewrite the entire passage changing the work <u>car</u> to <u>auto</u> (sentence 3).

3.   Rewrite the entire passage changing the words <u>a boy</u> to <u>a girl</u> (sentence 5).

4.   Rewrite the entire passage changing the words <u>a boy</u> to <u>two boys</u> (sentence 5).

7.   Rewrite the entire passage in the past tense. Begin sentence 1 with the word <u>Yesterday</u>.

24.   Rewrite the entire passage combining sentences 1 and 2 and sentences 6 and 7 using the word <u>who</u> or <u>which</u>.

Antibilingualism

[1]The sixties and seventies were the decades of bilingualism. [2]Bilingualism can be defined as the idea that government should provide education and services in languages other than English. [3]States such as Florida and California employ thousands of bilingual teachers and office workers. [4]Their Spanish-speaking populations are very large.

[5]The eighties saw a basic change in the country's attitude toward bilingualism. [6]Many states decided to protect English by law. [7]These states made English their official language. [8]Even Dade County, Florida, tried to protect English. [9]Half the population there speaks Spanish. [10]The change did not bother Miami-area Cubans and Cuban-Americans. [11]They said, "A law is one thing, but in fact, everyone in Miami wants to be bilingual."

[12]Maybe the new English-only laws do not affect people's lives in a day-to-day way. [13]But they have an emotional effect. [14]They only increase the separation among different language groups.

Steps

8. Pretend that all these things are happening right now. Rewrite the entire passage. Do not change paragraph 1, sentence 9, or the quotation in sentence 11. Your second paragraph will begin as follows:

    Right now we are seeing a basic change in the country's attitude toward bilingualism.

10. Pretend that all these things have happened recently. Rewrite the entire passage in the form that uses <u>have</u> or <u>has</u> in front of every main verb. Do not change paragraph 1, sentence 9, or the quotation in sentence 11. Your second paragraph will begin as follows:

    Recently we have seen a basic change in the country's attitude toward bilingualism.

24. Rewrite the entire passage combining sentences 1 and 2, sentences 3 and 4, sentences 6 and 7, sentences 8 and 9, sentences 10 and 11, and sentences 13 and 14 with words like <u>who</u>, <u>which</u>, <u>whose</u>, and <u>where</u>. Remember that sometimes you must put one sentence *inside* the other to make the new sentence sound correct.

Big Business

¹Federico Alvear, a 57-year-old lawyer from Venezuela, says that he owns the moon and has a deed to prove it.   ²He points out that the law in his country permits anyone to take ownership of property that has not already been claimed.   ³In 1953 he claimed the moon and obtained a deed.

⁴Mr. Alvear wants to meet the astronauts who have explored the moon.   ⁵He says he will give them official permission to continue these expeditions of importance.   ⁶He will also discuss with them possibilities for settlements on the moon.

⁷Mr. Alvear goes on to say that he has not paid any taxes on his property.   ⁸Several years ago, he was asked to pay, but he said he did not know the value of the land.   ⁹He suggested that some tax officials with plenty of courage go and survey the moon themselves.

¹⁰Mr. Alvear feels that his claim, which was once treated as a joke among his neighbors, is serious business.   ¹¹He says that many people have called him crazy, but no one has called him stupid.

Steps

11. Pretend that you are writing in the year 2000 and reporting something that happened a short while ago. Rewrite the entire passage beginning with the following sentence:

    Recently Federico Alvear, a 57-year-old lawyer from Venezuela, said that he owned the moon and had a deed to prove it.

14. Rewrite the entire passage changing all reported speech to direct speech. Decide what the speaker's exact words are and put quotation marks around them. Your first sentence will be as follows:

    Federico Alvear, a 57-year-old lawyer from Venezuela, says, "I own the moon and have a deed to prove it.

19. Underline the following phrases and clauses: from Venezuela (sentence 1), that has not already been claimed (sentence 2), of importance (sentence 5), with plenty of courage (sentence 9), and among his neighbors (sentence 10). Then rewrite the entire passage changing the key word(s) in each phrase or clause to a *new form*. Place that form in front of the noun that the phrase or clause originally followed.

Block Associations

¹Several years ago, residents of New York City took action to solve their problems of safety and sanitation. ²Concerned neighbors formed block associations to improve local conditions.

³The block associations decided to clean up and beautify the streets, to make them more secure, and to get merchants' cooperation in their attempts at self-renewal. ⁴The members of the associations collected money to put up better lights for increased safety during the nighttime. ⁵They bought trees and plants for the sidewalks and entrances to buildings. ⁶They petitioned neighborhood food stores to improve cleanliness, pricing, and service to customers. ⁷Some block associations even organized patrols of two persons to walk the streets after dark.

⁸Naturally, some residents ignored the efforts of their block associations. ⁹However, pressure from the neighborhood began to draw more and more people into the associations, and many residents found this involvement a pleasure.

Steps

8. Pretend that all the things in the passage above are happening right now. Rewrite the entire passage in the tense that uses a form of BE in front of every main verb and -ing after it. Begin with the following sentence:

    Right now, residents of New York City are taking action to solve their problems of safety and sanitation.

10. Rewrite the entire passage in the form that uses have or has in front of every main verb. Your first sentence will be as follows:

    During the past several years, residents of New York City have taken action to solve their problems of safety and sanitation.

18. Underline the following phrases: of New York City (sentence 1), at self-renewal (sentence 3), of the association and during the nighttime (sentence 4), to buildings (sentence 5), of two persons (sentence 7), and from the neighborhood (sentence 9).

    Pick out the most important word in each phrase and circle it. Then if any of the circled words are plural, make them singular. If you need two words instead of one, hyphenate them. Here are two examples:

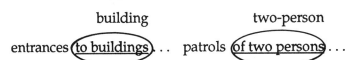

Continued

4

Steps

Finally, rewrite the entire passage placing each of the words that you have formed from a phrase in front of the noun that each phrase originally followed. Your first sentence will be as follows:

Several years ago, New York City residents took action to solve their problems of safety and sanitation.

Blue Collar

[1]According to the American stereotype, blue-collar workers are people with little formal education who use their muscles instead of their brains to earn a living. [2]They come home from work, open a can of beer, sit down, and start complaining about work, money, and demands made by minority groups.

[3]This stereotype, which has wide acceptance throughout the country, is unfair. [4]Blue-collar workers have to use both mind and body. Often their jobs require a good deal of knowledge and skill. [5]As a rule, blue-collar workers enter the work force right after high school. [6]If they want more education, they pay for it themselves, without the support of families or scholarships.

[7]If blue-collar workers complain, there *are* some good reasons. [8]Their bosses tell them that they are the laborers with the highest pay in history. But the workers look around and see that the gap between the rich and the poor is wider than ever. [9]They feel that the government has ignored them in favor of welfare clients on the one hand and interests of corporations on the other. [10]Blue-collar workers consider themselves forgotten people.

Steps

5.	Rewrite the entire passage changing the words <u>blue-collar workers</u> to <u>the blue-collar worker</u> wherever they appear. You will be writing about one person instead of many people throughout your composition. Your first sentence will be as follows:

> According to the American stereotype, the blue-collar worker is a person with little formal education who uses his or her muscles instead of his or her brains to earn a living.

> *Note:* This step requires more than 40 changes.

7.	Pretend that you are writing in the twenty-first century when the image of blue-collar workers has changed. Rewrite the entire passage beginning with the following sentence:

> According to the twentieth-century American stereotype, blue-collar workers were people with little formal education who used their muscles instead of their brains to earn a living.

20.	Change the underlined phrases and clauses to one or two words or to hyphenated words. Then place the new word(s) in front of the noun that the phrase or clause originally followed: <u>made by minority groups</u> (sentence 2), <u>which has wide acceptance</u> (sentence 3), <u>of families</u> (sentence 6), <u>with the highest pay</u> (sentence 8), and <u>of corporations</u> (sentence 9).

Bureaucracy

[1]An evil force does not create bureaucracies. [2]Human beings create them. [3]Believe it or not, one man started the giant Ford Motor Company. [4]You can take any other large corporation or government agency as an example.

[5]In the beginning, perhaps, an individual sets up an office. [6]Then, he hires employees, expands the operation, and hires more employees. [7]Soon, size and impersonality break the human ties among workers.

[8]In a full-grown bureaucracy, bosses seldom trust workers. [9]They require their workers to clock in. [10]They forget people's names. [11]Memos replace face-to-face communication. [12]Mountains of paperwork reduce efficiency. [13]Managers divide labor into small bits. [14]The workers themselves do not see the final results of their labor. [15]This situation, in turn, affects their attitudes. [16]They say to themselves, "Why bother? I'm just a cog in a machine."

Steps

1. Copy the entire passage.

15. Rewrite the entire passage changing all sentences from the active voice to the passive voice. Follow the example below:

| ACTIVE | The dog | bit | the man. |
| PASSIVE | The man | was bitten | by the dog. |

If the phrase beginning with by seems unnecessary, leave it out, as in the following example:

| ACTIVE | Police | arrested | the thief. |
| PASSIVE | The thief | was arrested | (by the police). |

In this composition, your first sentence will be as follows:

Bureaucracies are not created by an evil force.

Note: Do not change sentence 16.

Cancerians

[1]A Cancerian, who is someone born between June 21 and July 21, has certain characteristics.   [2]Born under the sign of the Crab, he is a person who loves peace.   [3]He has a quiet, sensitive, and gentle nature.   [4]However, he is able to defend himself if necessary.   [5]His memory is excellent, and he enjoys research into history.   [6]When he makes plans, he sees them through tenaciously.

[7]Although a Cancerian prefers a life of solitude, he excels in work where he can care for others.   [8]People trust him more than he trusts himself.   [9]In love, he is protective, sacrificing, and romantic.   [10]He seeks and needs security in anything having to do with the emotions.   [11]He enjoys chores around the house and makes a responsible parent.

[12]A Cancerian's weaknesses are timidity, moodiness, and feelings of inferiority.   [13]He sometimes experiences fears without reason.   [14]He has to avoid stress and learn the art of relaxation of the muscles.   [15]Because of these traits, yoga and meditation are useful pastimes for him.

Steps

3. Rewrite the entire passage adding the word <u>woman</u> after the word <u>Cancerian</u> wherever it appears. You will be writing about a woman throughout your composition. Be sure to put the apostrophe in the correct place when you come to the word <u>Cancerian's</u> in sentence 12. Your first two sentences will be as follows:

   A Cancerian woman, who is someone born between June 21 and July 21, has certain characteristics. Born under the sign of the Crab, she is a person who loves peace.

6. Pretend that this passage is a prediction about the future of a newborn baby. Rewrite the entire passage using <u>will</u> at least once in every sentence. Your first two sentences will be as follows:

   If a baby is born between June 21 and July 21, he will be a Cancerian and have certain characteristics. Born under the sign of the Crab, he will be a person who loves peace.

19. Underline the following phrases and clauses: <u>who loves peace</u> (sentence 2), <u>into history</u> (sentence 5), <u>of solitude</u> (sentence 7), <u>in anything having to do with the emotions</u> (sentence 10), <u>around the house</u> (sentence 11), <u>without reason</u> (sentence 13), and <u>of the muscles</u> (sentence 14). Then rewrite the entire passage, changing the key word(s) in each phrase or clause to a *new form*. Place that form in front of the noun that the phrase or clause originally followed.

Capricornians

[1]Capricornians are people who were born under the zodiac sign of the Goat (December 21 to January 19).   [2]Like the goat, they are tough, stubborn individuals who can make do with almost anything that comes their way.

[3]Capricornians get down to business and work hard.   [4]They also do the best job they can.   [5]They are natural administrators.   [6]They carry the burden of responsibility well.   [7]Others respect them for their practicality, shrewd business sense, and organizing abilities.

[8]Capricornians approach love and marriage in the same way as they approach business.   [9]They make faithful marriage partners.   [10]However, they do not make passionate lovers.   [11]They expect their spouses' commitment to be as strong as their own.   [12]Unfortunately, they have a tendency to keep their emotions to themselves.   [13]For this reason, they sometimes seem cold and unfeeling.

Steps

1.   Copy the entire passage.

5.   Rewrite the entire passage changing the word Capricornians to a Capricornian wherever it appears. Your first sentence will be as follows:

   A Capricornian is a person who was born under the zodiac sign of the Goat (December 21 to January 19).

23.   Rewrite the entire passage combining sentences 3 and 4, sentences 5 and 6, sentences 9 and 10, and sentences 12 and 13 with words like and, but, and so. Leave out the word However, in sentence 10 and the words For this reason, in sentence 13.

   Remember to *make your new sentences as short and clear as possible.* If you join two sentences having the same subject (or some other part), do not repeat the subject (or part) in the combined sentence.

Central Park

[1]Every Sunday during the summer, Central Park comes alive. [2]People enjoy themselves and forget about their own and the city's problems.

[3]The main drive fills up with bicycle riders. [4]Some of them race one another. [5]Other cyclists get in shape by slower, steadier pedaling. [6]The joggers on the drive work up a sweat by running around the reservoir. [7]An army of young baseball players gathers on the big lawn to prepare for practice. [8]Frisbee players warm up. [9]They use the fringes of the lawn. [10]A Jamaican steel band plays an ear-catching tune near the lake. [11]The lake is invaded by amateur boaters. [12]Dog walkers chat with one another and exchange dog stories. [13]Their animals sniff every bush and tree.

[14]Hundreds of people walk, talk, sunbathe, or just sit around on the benches. [15]The benches begin to look like subway seats with all the crowding. [16]No one objects. [17]Everyone has too much fun to complain.

Steps

2.   Rewrite the entire passage changing the following words: problems to troubles (sentence 2), sweat to appetite (sentence 6), army to troop (sentence 7), ear-catching to lively (sentence 10), animals to beasts (sentence 13), and look like to resemble (sentence 15).

8.   Pretend that all the things in the passage above are happening right now. Rewrite the entire passage in the tense that uses a form of BE in front of every main verb and -ing after it. Begin with the following sentence:

Right now Central Park is coming alive.

24.   Rewrite the entire passage combining sentences 1 and 2, sentences 3 and 4, sentences 8 and 9, sentences 10 and 11, sentences 12 and 13, and sentences 14 and 15 using words like who, which, that, whose, and where. Sometimes you may have to put one sentence *inside* the other to make the new sentence sound correct. Your first sentence will be as follows:

Every Sunday during the summer, Central Park, where people enjoy themselves and forget about their own and the city's problems, comes alive.

Changing Roles

¹Is there any reason to be optimistic about marriage and the family in America? ²The answer is yes, and the main reason is that many changes are taking place in the roles of husbands and wives.

³The wife is not satisfied with the idea that she will be staying home the rest of her life. ⁴Even if she enjoys housework and taking care of children, she sees herself as more than a housekeeper and mother. ⁵She is looking for ways to establish her own identity. ⁶If she gets a job, she does not have to apologize for working. ⁷Being able to rely on herself is of great importance to her.

⁸The husband's role is changing, too. ⁹He is beginning to realize that work should not be the most important thing in his life. ¹⁰He understands that he must share family responsibilities if he wants to be an equal partner. ¹¹The idea of washing dishes and changing diapers does not bother him, and he does not consider himself henpecked for doing what is sometimes called women's work.

Steps

4. Rewrite the entire passage changing the word <u>wife</u> to <u>wives</u> and the word <u>husband</u> to <u>husbands</u> wherever they appear. You will be writing about many wives and husbands instead of one of each throughout your composition. Your second paragraph will begin as follows:

   Wives are not satisfied with the idea that they will be staying home the rest of their lives.

10. Pretend that these changes in roles have already taken place. Rewrite the entire passage in the form that uses <u>have</u> or <u>has</u> in front of every main verb. Do not change the first part of sentence 7. Your first paragraph will begin as follows:

    Has there been any reason to be optimistic about the future of marriage and the family in America? The answer is yes, and the main reason is that many changes have taken place in the roles of husbands and wives.

21. Rewrite the entire passage using the words below to replace *two or more words* in the indicated sentences.

sentence 3: prospect	sentence 7: crucial
sentence 4: childcare	sentence 9: paramount
sentence 7: self-reliance	sentence 11: so-called

    Remember to add a small word like <u>the</u> or <u>is</u>, if necessary, to make the new word(s) fit in correctly.

Coffee Breakthrough

[1]Tina Reed is an executive assistant in a large advertising firm. [2]Last week she challenged her boss on a small but important issue. [3]He threatened to fire her if she insisted on having her own way. [4]She took the matter to the company's personnel director. [5]The director spoke to the two employees. [6]He got this story:

[7]"Mr. Ames told me that I would have to make coffee for him every morning," said the 22-year-old Ms. Reed, "but I refused. [8]I don't feel that making coffee is part of my job."

[9]Mr. Ames insisted he was not being unreasonable. [10]He simply wanted his coffee. [11]The personnel director asked him why he couldn't make it himself. [12]"I can," he answered, "but my time is too valuable for things like that."

[13]The director felt that both employees' time was too valuable for making coffee. [14]He suggested that they send a messenger to the cafeteria. [15]He added, "I just hope that we can still find a messenger who doesn't feel it's beneath his—or her—dignity to run errands."

Steps

1. Copy the entire passage, including the title. Remember to leave out the sentence numbers 1-15.

26. Rewrite the entire passage. Combine sentences 1 and 2, sentences 3 and 4, sentences 5 and 6, sentences 7 and 8, sentences 9 and 10, and sentences 13, 14, and 15 in the *shortest and clearest way possible*. Don't leave out any of the information.

Colleges Today

[1]Years ago, colleges were seen as ivy-covered centers of knowledge with little practical value. [2]College students were considered an elite group because opportunities for education were limited by factors of social status and economics. [3]They were envied by many and dismissed by others as living a safe, sheltered life, separate from the real world.

[4]Today the "halls of ivy" picture of college has been replaced by a new image. [5]Students are attracted by the promise of practical training oriented toward jobs. [6]The liberal arts have been deemphasized. [7]Many new colleges without residences and community colleges have been established for urban students, and entrance requirements have been changed to admit students needing basic skills help.

[8]How will colleges be seen in the years to come? [9]How will the arts and sciences be brought together? [10]The marriage of the classical and the practical can be accomplished only if college subjects are used to make sense of the whole world. [11]For example, poetry can explain both love and hate; history can tell us how to live in the present. [12]College life should be real life, not an escape from it or a narrow preparation for it.

Steps

16. Rewrite the entire passage in the active voice, except sentences 11 and 12. Remember that you will need a new subject for each sentence or each part of a sentence that you change. Look for phrases starting with <u>by</u> for your new subject or create your own subject. Your first sentence will be as follows:

    Years ago, people saw colleges as ivy-covered centers of knowledge with little practical value.

19. Underline the following phrases and clauses: <u>with little practical value</u> (sentence 1), <u>for education</u> (sentence 2), <u>of social status and economics</u> (sentence 2), <u>oriented toward jobs</u> (sentence 5), <u>without residences</u> (sentence 7), and <u>to come</u> (sentence 8). Then rewrite the entire passage changing the key word(s) in each phrase or clause to a *new form*. Place that form in front of the noun that the phrase or clause originally followed.

Detectives

[1]When I was nine years old, I imagined that I was every detective on TV. [2] I didn't wear a jacket with my suit at the time, so my toy gun and holster were under my shirt making a bulge as big as a cantaloupe. [3]I never felt silly. [4]I was sure that I was the best detective on foot ever. I have thought many times since then about what makes the life of a detective so attractive.

[5]For one thing, a detective solves crimes, and other grown-ups do not. [6]Other grown-ups live with crime and complain. [7]Second, a detective has a mission with multiple purposes: to look for, to find, and to turn over the criminal to the authorities. [8]He is both an idealist and a realist. [9]He thinks he can improve the world of everyday by catching a murderer, but he knows that the improvement lasts only until the next crime. [10]He also knows right from wrong and acts on the difference. At the same time, he lives in mystery with style. [11]Perhaps that mystery is his greatest appeal.

[12]Very few people are cut out to be detectives. [13]I found out quite early that I was not one of them. [14]Now I walk the streets late at night, knowing that the person following me is actually the detective of my imagination.

Steps

2. Rewrite the entire passage changing the words cantaloupe to eggplant (sentence 2), multiple to several (sentence 7), idealist to romantic (sentence 8), murderer to killer (sentence 9), cut out to suited (sentence 12), found out to discovered (sentence 13), imagination to mind (sentence 14).

4. Rewrite the entire passage changing *only the second paragraph*. In that paragraph, change the words a detective to detectives wherever they appear. This means that you will be writing about many detectives instead of just one throughout your composition. The first sentence in your second paragraph will begin as follows:

   For one thing, detectives solve crimes, and other grown-ups do not.

18. Underline the following phrases: on TV (sentence 1), with my suit (sentence 2), on foot (sentence 4), with multiple purposes (sentence 7), of everyday (sentence 9), and late at night (sentence 14). Then rewrite the entire passage replacing each of the underlined phrases with single or hyphenated words placed in front of the noun that each phrase originally followed.

Don't Run Away

¹Recently while walking in the park, I unexpectedly crossed the finish line of a marathon for nonprofessional runners. ²Seeing the mixture of exhaustion and exhilaration the runners displayed, I was curious. I decided to ask these people what made them run. Here is what each person replied:

An accountant:	³To me, it's a simple matter of keeping my body in as good condition as possible. ⁴If I don't run, my middle will spread like a beanbag.
A philosopher:	⁵How else can one put together mind and body, pain and pleasure so simply? ⁶Running is a way of bringing inner conflict to an end.
A musician:	⁷Running has made it possible for me to hear the rhythm of my own body.
A lawyer:	⁸Are you kidding? ⁹Once I weighed 240 pounds. ¹⁰Running beats any diet on earth!
An actress:	¹¹I'm more aware of my body in a close and familiar way. ¹²Running helps me be more sensitive and expressive in my acting.
An adventurer:	¹³I feel that anyone who has become an adult will seek new challenges.
A writer:	¹⁴My therapist is a runner, too. ¹⁵He is always telling me not to run away from minor fears and worries—just to run!

Steps

12. Rewrite the entire passage in two paragraphs using reported speech. Your second paragraph will begin as follows:

> An accountant said that to him it was a simple matter of keeping his body in as good condition as possible.

13. Rewrite the entire passage changing each portion of dialog into a separate paragraph of direct speech. Remember to add quotation marks, commas, and phrases such as <u>An accountant said</u> to your composition. Your second paragraph will begin as follows:

> An accountant said," To me, it's a simple matter of keeping my body in as good condition as possible.

Continued

Steps

22. Rewrite the entire passage condensing the sentences indicated below by replacing several words in each with *one* of the given word forms.

sentence 1: amateur/amateurs   sentence 11: intimate/intimately/intimacy

sentence 3: fit/fitness   sentence 13: mature/matured/maturity

sentence 6: resolving/resolution   sentence 15: anxious/anxiety/anxieties

sentence 7: enable/enabled

Fire Alarm

¹A fire alarm rang on 75th Street. ²Suddenly everything went haywire. ³Mrs. Miles climbed on her chair on the stoop. ⁴Her neighbor ran out to join her. ⁵Several motorists stopped their cars in the middle of the street, blocking traffic.

⁶Mrs. Stern picked up her grocery cart in her arms. ⁷Louie, one of the neighborhood boys, fell off his bicycle into a trash barrel. ⁸The mail carrier was very distracted by the confusion. ⁹He bumped into everyone in his way.

¹⁰Mrs. Santiago's three dogs filled the air with howling. ¹¹They wrapped up her legs with their leashes. ¹²One passerby covered his head with a newspaper while another one raced into a phone booth.

¹³To top off all the confusion, the fire engine was held up at the corner because of the stopped cars. ¹⁴The firemen yelled and motioned. ¹⁵No one paid any attention to them. ¹⁶What a mess!

Steps

8. Pretend that these things are happening right now. Rewrite the entire passage beginning with the following sentence:

   At this moment, a fire alarm is ringing on 75th Street.

10. Rewrite the entire passage in the form that uses <u>have</u> or <u>has</u> in front of every main verb. Your first sentence will begin as follows:

   A fire alarm has just rung on 75th Street.

23. Rewrite the entire passage combining sentences 1 and 2, sentences 3 and 4, sentences 8 and 9, sentences 10 and 11, and sentences 14 and 15 with the words <u>and</u>, <u>but</u>, or <u>so</u>.

   Remember to make your new sentences as clear and concise as possible.

Fire and I

¹I have seen that fire and I have a lot in common.   ²I can show this to be true by means of the opposite qualities we share: assertion and yielding, beauty and ugliness.

³Fire is both assertive and yielding, and so am I.   ⁴Fire is a powerful force when it burns freely.   ⁵However, it must yield to water or a shortage of oxygen.   ⁶I am a normal, healthy individual.   ⁷Therefore, I have physical and emotional strength.   ⁸I assert myself in an argument and in my work.   ⁹But I have weaknesses, too.   ¹⁰One of these is yielding to the colorful temptations around me in city life.

¹¹Fire is beautiful and ugly, and sometimes I am, too.   ¹²Firecrackers going off on the Fourth of July are beautiful.   ¹³So is a campfire or crackling logs in a fireplace.   ¹⁴But sometimes fire erupts in a house or a forest.   ¹⁵Then it looks like an ugly monster.   ¹⁶I feel beautiful when I do something kind, but my bad temper makes me feel ugly.   ¹⁷It can make me blow up in a moment.

¹⁸Everything in nature is related.   ¹⁹Everything shares the opposites. ²⁰I feel less alone, more at peace with the world, through seeing this.

Steps

2.   Rewrite the entire passage changing the words <u>seen</u> to <u>noticed</u> (sentence 1), <u>show</u> to <u>demonstrate</u> (sentence 2), <u>powerful</u> to <u>imposing</u> (sentence 4), <u>shortage</u> to <u>absence</u> (sentence 5), <u>normal</u> to <u>sane</u> (sentence 6), <u>argument</u> to <u>dispute</u> (sentence 8), <u>going off</u> to <u>exploding</u> (sentence 12), <u>house</u> to <u>apartment</u> (sentence 14), <u>ugly</u> to <u>horrible</u> (sentence 15), and <u>moment</u> to <u>instant</u> (sentence 17).

5.   The passage above is based on a composition written by a student named Kam Sing Au. Rewrite the entire passage using the student's name Mr. Au in sentences 6, 15, and 19. Change <u>I</u> to <u>he</u> elsewhere. Your first sentence will be as follows:

   Kam Sing Au has seen that he and fire have a lot in common.

Continued

25. Rewrite the entire passage combining sentences 1 and 2, sentences 4 and 5, sentences 6 and 7, sentences 9 and 10, sentences 14 and15, sentences 16 and 17, and sentences 18 and 19 using words like <u>which,</u> <u>who,</u> and <u>whose,</u> (as in Step 24) or <u>when,</u> <u>although,</u> and <u>because</u> to form adverbial clauses. Leave out the following words as you combine: <u>However,</u> (sentence 5), <u>Therefore,</u> (sentence 7), <u>sometimes</u> (sentence 14) and <u>Then</u> (sentence 15). Your first sentence will be as follows:

    I have seen that fire and I have a lot in common, which I can show to be true by means of the opposite qualities we share: assertion and yielding, beauty and ugliness.

Give it Up

¹Smoking seems to give pleasure to many people.   ²Habit alone can keep people smoking.   ³However, many heavy smokers offer other reasons for their actions.

⁴Right now doctors are receiving alot of attention in their protests against heavy smoking.   ⁵Many people have cut down on their smoking or have stopped completely.   ⁶In general, almost everyone believes the doctors' warnings.

⁷It is sometimes very easy to stop smoking.   ⁸For example, at a party a man decides he will have just one cigarette.   ⁹He makes himself stop thinking about having another one.   ¹⁰Both health considerations and the expense of smoking help him to stay away from tobacco.   ¹¹All his friends help, too.   ¹²They always understand his problem and want to give him encouragement.   ¹³The heavy smoker needs friends like these.

Steps

17.   Rewrite the entire passage changing each sentence from the affirmative to the negative so that your composition states just the opposite of what the model passage says. In some sentences, you can simply add the word not. In others, you will need other negative words like no, never, no one, neither, and nor. Your first sentence will be one of the following examples:

Smoking does not seem to give pleasure to many people.

or

Smoking seems to give pleasure to no one.

25.   Rewrite the entire passage combining sentences 2 and 3, sentences 5 and 6, sentences 8 and 9, and sentences 11 and 12 using words like if, when, although, because, and after to form adverbial clauses. Leave out the word However, in sentence 3.

A Good Friend

[1]Everyone wants a friend who encourages the best in him.   [2]Such a friend shows he is interested in strengthening another.   [3]He can be counted on to give his support.   [4]He will criticize, too, because he knows a person has to have feedback to grow and change.

[5]A good friend thinks carefully before he criticizes.   [6]He always asks himself whether his criticism is fair.   [7]He tries to find out all the facts involved in a situation because he knows how harmful inaccuracy can be.

[8]Kindness is also important to him.   [9]He wants to understand what the other person is feeling and to respect those feelings.   [10]He is always willing to criticize himself when needed, and he makes every effort to avoid sounding smug or self-righteous.

[11]If a friend is both accurate and kind as a critic, everyone respects what he says.   [12]His criticism is something like love.

Steps

3. Imagine that the critical friend in the passage above is a woman instead of a man. Rewrite the entire passage changing the word <u>he</u> to <u>she</u> and making all other changes that will show the critic to be a woman. Your first two sentences will be as follows:

    Everyone wants a friend who encourages the best in him. Such a friend shows she is interested in strengthening another.

17. Imagine that the person in the passage above is not a good friend at all. Rather, he is an uncaring individual who does not encourage or criticize or, if he does criticize, does it badly. Rewrite the entire passage changing the words <u>a good friend</u> to <u>a bad friend</u> where they appear in the title and in sentence 4. Change every sentence from the affirmative to the negative by using words like <u>not</u>, <u>never</u>, <u>neither</u>, and <u>nor</u>. Your first sentence will be as follows:

    No one wants a friend who doesn't encourage the best in him.

    Remember that not every verb must be negative. If a sentence has more than one verb, you should change whatever part or parts of the sentence will make it sound the way it should.

Continued

21

Steps

21. Rewrite the entire passage using the words below to replace *two or more words* in the indicated sentences:

sentence 2: supportive

sentence 4: develop

sentence 6: questions

sentence 7: researches

sentence 10: self-critical

sentence 10: endeavors

Remember to add a small word like <u>the</u> or <u>is</u>, if necessary, to make the new word(s) fit correctly.

Guest of Honor

¹In his book *Dracula*, Bram Stoker writes about a famous count who was really a vampire.   ²This man lived on the blood of his victims. Here is a part of his story:

³At midday an air of activity filled the Marsden estate.   ⁴Lady Marsden was giving crisp orders, and everyone was making preparations for a lawn party.

⁵At 3:00 the butler received the first guests and conducted them to the patio.

⁶At 4:00 guests filled the patio and lawn, and Lady Marsden told them about a surprise guest of honor and asked them to wait patiently for his arrival.

⁷At 6:00 the guests showed clear displeasure over the delay.   ⁸They drank all the punch and ate the little tea cakes grumblingly.   ⁹Someone started an unkind rumor about the missing guest of honor and Lady Marsden.

¹⁰At sundown everyone noticed a chill in the air.   ¹¹Deep shadows blanketed the lawn, and strange tapestries of dark and light draped the trees. ¹²As soon as darkness covered all, Lady Marsden announced the arrival of the guest of honor.   ¹³She introduced the mysterious count and made apologies for his lateness.

¹⁴At midnight the count became the life of the party — in fact, the only life.   ¹⁵In case you haven't guessed, the guest of honor was Count Dracula.

Steps

6.   Pretend that you are a fortune teller telling this story. Rewrite the entire passage, except the first paragraph, in the future tense using <u>will</u>. The first sentence of the second paragraph will be as follows:

   At midday an air of activity will fill the Marsden estate.

9.   Rewrite the entire passage, except the first paragraph, in the form that uses <u>had</u> in front of every main verb. Change the word <u>At</u> to <u>By</u> at the beginning of each paragraph and the phrase <u>As soon as</u> to <u>By the time</u> in sentence 12. Do not change sentence 15. The first sentence of the second paragraph will be as follows:

   By midday an air of activity had filled the Marsden estate.

15.   Rewrite the entire passage, except the first paragraph, in the passive voice. Change all sentences *except 14 and 15.*. The first sentence of the second paragraph will be as follows:

   At midday the Marsden estate was filled with an air of activity.

Keep a Cat

¹In many big cities, people own cats. ²Although cats that live in stores or restaurants are useful for catching rats and mice, cats that live in apartments don't do a thing to earn their living. ³Why, then, do so many people who live in cities keep cats?

⁴First, cats relieve the loneliness that many city dwellers feel. ⁵They are bright, loving, and active. ⁶Their ability to entertain is almost unlimited.

⁷Second, cats are easy to take care of. ⁸They don't have to be washed, walked, or licensed, and they seem to be able to entertain themselves during long hours alone. ⁹All they need is food, water, and affection supplied on a regular basis.

¹⁰In spite of all this, cats are not just docile balls of fur. ¹¹They demand respect. ¹²Their swishing tails warn dogs that visit that they are displeased, and they can attack quite viciously. ¹³Even in play, cat lovers have to be careful. ¹⁴Although bites from cats are generally just little nips, cats have claws as sharp as razors, and "play" can often draw blood. ¹⁵Some cat owners admit that they like this viciousness; they are glad that cats are not pushovers.

Steps

5. Rewrite the entire passage changing the word <u>cats</u> to <u>a cat</u> wherever it appears. You will be writing about one cat instead of many, and you should call the cat "he" or "she" but only *one* of those words. Your first sentence will be as follows:

   In many big cities, people own a cat.

7. Pretend that you are living at a time far in the future when cats are no longer known. Rewrite the entire passage in the past tense. Your first sentence will be as follows:

   During the twentieth century, people in many big cities owned cats.

Continued

Steps

20. This step is very similar to Steps 18 and 19. Once again, you will have to take the meaning from a phrase or clause *following* a noun and turn it into hyphenated words or one or two words that can go *in front of* the same noun. Sometimes you may need a possessive ending (-'s or -s') to make your new words, or an -ly ending added to the first of two words, as in *carefully written*. Rewrite the entire passage changing the following phrases and clauses as before: who live in cities (sentence 3), many city dwellers feel (sentence 4), on a regular basis (sentence 9), who visits (sentence 12), from cats (sentence 14), and as sharp as razors (sentence 14).

Late Night City

¹Even after midnight the city still throbs with activity. ²The bars and restaurants do a good business because many people eat a complete meal after a movie or show. ³In newspaper offices, reporters and other staff members rush to meet deadlines. ⁴Telephones ring, and printing presses turn noisily. ⁵In the city hospitals, night nurses make the usual rounds. ⁶Ambulances pick up and drop off patients, and emergency cases are treated by the night staff. ⁷The subway and buses run on an infrequent schedule, but riders use them anyway.

⁸An interesting variety of people move up and down the night streets. ⁹Some of them look for good places to sleep. ¹⁰Others wander around out of boredom or curiosity. ¹¹The average thief or purse-snatcher doesn't sleep at this hour. ¹²He looks for a helpless victim. ¹³The cop on the night beat also looks around and tries to find the thief before an actual robbery.

¹⁴The darkness and bright lights do not discriminate. ¹⁵Rich and poor, good and bad—almost everyone takes advantage of the city's insomnia.

Steps

2. Rewrite the entire passage changing the words <u>good</u> to <u>excellent</u> and <u>complete</u> to <u>entire</u> (sentence 2), <u>drop off</u> to <u>deposit</u> (sentence 6), <u>infrequent</u> to <u>reduced</u> (sentence 7), <u>interesting</u> to <u>intriguing</u> (sentence 8), <u>helpless</u> to <u>defenseless</u> (sentence 12), and <u>actual</u> to <u>real</u> (sentence 13).

8. Pretend that all the things in the passage above are happening right now. Rewrite the entire passage beginning with the following sentence:

    It's midnight, but the city is still throbbing with activity.

    Remember that each sentence must have at least one <u>-ing</u> form.

Leaders

¹National leaders are chosen differently around the world. ²In the Soviet Union, the premier is chosen by the Communist party. ³In both the United States and Great Britain, leaders are elected by citizens called voters. ⁴The preferences of the citizens are expressed by the process of voting secretly.

⁵In Great Britain, the elections are arranged by Parliament. ⁶These elections take place at least once every five years. ⁷Very short notice is given by Parliament before election day, so campaigning is limited by time. ⁸Generally, the candidates themselves are not given a lot of attention by the parties. ⁹Instead, party differences are stressed.

¹⁰In the United States, great amounts of time and money are spent by the candidates. ¹¹A president is elected every four years on the first Tuesday in November. ¹²That day never changes. ¹³The voters are surrounded by campaign ads, posters, and flyers. ¹⁴All this publicity contributes to the buildup of individual candidates. ¹⁵The candidates are backed by their parties, but their success or failure is determined largely by their personal ability to attract followers.

Steps

16. Rewrite the entire passage in the active voice. Do not change sentence 6, part of sentence 11, and sentence 14. They are already in the active voice. Remember that each sentence or part of a sentence must have a new subject.

    Note: The word Parliament (sentence 5) refers to a governing body and is a singular noun.

22. Rewrite the entire passage condensing the sentences indicated below by replacing several words in each sentence with *one* of the given word forms.

    sentence 4: ballot/balloting   sentence 12: fixed/fixes
    sentence 7: advance/in advance   sentence 14: promote/promotion
    sentence 8: emphasis/emphasized   sentence 15: charisma/charismatic

24. Rewrite the entire passage combining sentences 3 and 4, sentences 5 and 6, sentences 11 and 12, and sentences 13 and 14 with words like who, which, and that. Leave out any words that seem unnecessary in the combination.

    Remember that one sentence may have to go *inside* the other to make the new sentence sound correct.

A Letter Home

¹A college student is writing to his parents during a break between semesters. ²These are some of the things he says in his letter home.

³First, he apologizes to his parents for writing so irregularly. ⁴He knows his letters have been few and short, but he hopes his parents understand how busy he has been during his first semester as a freshman in college.

⁵He goes on to thank them for encouraging him to make friends. ⁶A lot of freshmen have had problems with roommates, and he is grateful that he has not. ⁷He has not joined a fraternity because he feels he can mix with people more freely without the label of a fraternity.

⁸He has one suggestion for his parents concerning his sister Peggy's preparations for college. ⁹He feels she will adjust better if they are firmer about her habits of study. ¹⁰He regrets his own lack of seriousness during his years in high school and admits he is still struggling with self-discipline.

¹¹He urges his parents not to worry about him. ¹²He can't come home until the summer vacation because the trip of 3,000 miles is too expensive, but he promises that he will write again very soon.

Steps

11. Pretend that this letter was written several years ago. Rewrite the entire passage in the past tense, but do not change the word are in sentence 2. You will need to add past tense signals like did, was, were, could, had, and would throughout your composition. Your first two sentences will be as follows:

    A college student was writing to his parents during a break between semesters. These are some of the things he said in his letter home.

14. Rewrite the entire passage changing all reported speech to direct speech. You will have to decide which are the letter writer's exact words and put quotation marks around them. The first sentence in your second paragraph will be as follows:

    "First, I apologize to you for writing so irregularly.

18. Underline the following phrases: between semesters (sentence 1), in college (sentence 4), with roommates (sentence 6), of a fraternity (sentence 7), of study (sentence 9), in high school (sentence 10), and of 3,000 miles (sentence 12). Then rewrite the entire passage replacing each of the underlined phrases with single or hyphenated words placed in front of the noun that each phrase originally followed.

Librans

[1]A Libran is someone born between September 22 and October 22.   [2]His sign of the zodiac is the Scales.   [3]The Scales represent justice.   [4]A Libran loves harmony and justice.   [5]He has compassion for all who suffer.   [6]This makes him well-suited for a career in medicine, law, or social work.   [7]He can also expect success in business.   [8]He gets along well with people and always sees both sides of a dispute.

[9]Venus is the ruling planet for a Libran.   [10]It gives the Libran consciousness of fashions and good taste in clothes, furnishings, and luxury goods.   [11]It also gives him another job possibility, that of an expert in beauty culture.

[12]A Libran is an affectionate partner in marriage.   [13]However, he must guard against seeming fickle.   [14]Sometimes he shows an interest of a romantic nature in another person.   [15]His partner may become furious. [16]The Libran may think he can handle more than one intimate relationship, but there is great danger.   [17]He should not overestimate himself in such matters.

Steps

4.   Rewrite the entire passage changing the words <u>a Libran</u> or <u>the Libran</u> to <u>Librans</u> wherever they appear. You will be writing about many Librans instead of just one. Your first two sentences will be as follows:

Librans are people born between September 22 and October 22. Their sign of the zodiac is the Scales.

18.   Underline the following phrases: <u>of the zodiac</u> (sentence 2), <u>in business</u> (sentence 7), <u>of fashions</u> (sentence 10), <u>in beauty culture</u> (sentence 11), <u>in marriage</u> (sentence 12), <u>of a romantic nature</u> (sentence 14). Then rewrite the entire passage replacing each of the underlined phrases with single or hyphenated words placed in front of the noun that each phrase originally followed.

Remember to change a plural noun to its singular form if it precedes another noun.

25.   Rewrite the entire passage combining sentences 2 and 3, sentences 4 and 5, sentences 7 and 8, sentences 9 and 10, sentences 12 and 13, and sentences 14 and 15 using words like <u>which, who,</u> and <u>whose</u>, or <u>when, although,</u> and <u>because</u> to form adverbial clauses. Leave out any unnecessary words, for example, <u>However,</u> in sentence 13.

The Light-Fingered Elephant

¹Petal, the Philadelphia Zoo's 15-year-old African elephant, thought zookeeper Ed Recotta had some candy in his pocket. ²Many zookeepers do carry candy, and the elephants just help themselves to the snack with their trunks while the zookeepers clean their cages. ³Yesterday Petal's "snack" was Recotta's weekly paycheck.

⁴"I was hanging on her trunk trying to get it out of her mouth when help came," said Recotta. ⁵Unfortunately, the check had already disappeared inside the four-ton animal. ⁶Zoo officials wrote Recotta another check later that day, but the banks had closed, so he had to find himself a check-cashing place.

⁷Can you imagine this scene? ⁸The zookeeper comes home late, and his wife says, "You're late. Where have you been?"

⁹The unfortunate man replies, "I couldn't help it. An elephant swallowed my paycheck!"

Steps

1. Copy the entire passage, from the first word in the title to the last word in sentence 9, paycheck. Do not copy the sentence numbers 1–9, but copy everything else exactly as it is. When you finish this first composition, immediately give it to your teacher to read. Do not go on to step 3 below. Your teacher will mark your paper and tell you what to do next by writing the title of another passage at the top of your composition.

3. Pretend that all zookeepers are women. Rewrite the entire passage changing the name Ed Recotta to Edith Recotta in the first pragraph so that you will be writing about a woman throughout your composition. Your first sentence will be as follows:

   Petal, the Philadelphia Zoo's 15-year-old African elephant, thought zookeeper Edith Recotta had some candy in her pocket.

Manhattan Green

[1]People sometimes call Manhattan a forest of glass and steel. [2]However, any interested person can find real trees on many Manhattan streets. [3]People like George Bassat of West 85th Street acquire and take care of them. [4]This is how he does it:

February: [5]A sincere wish to improve the neighborhood prompts George to look into the possibility of planting trees. [6]He contacts the local block association. [7]The block association sends him a list of public-spirited merchants.

March: [8]George encourages the merchants to contribute to the new tree fund. [9]Some merchants give generous amounts, and George appreciates every sum. [10]He asks everyone on the block to contribute ten dollars. [11]A few people ignore the request altogether, but most greet the idea enthusiastically.

April: [12]Finally the fund reaches the necessary amount. [13]George calls a nursery and orders 30 trees. [14]The nurserymen bring the trees and dig out 30 squares of concrete. [15]They plant the trees and water them thoroughly.

May: [16]George puts up signs saying Curb your dog and Please water me. [17]The trees make people a little happier, and George adds one more sign: Smile! You are in a friendly neighborhood.

Steps

10. Rewrite the entire passage in the form that uses <u>have</u> or <u>has</u> in front of every main verb. Do not change anything written on the signs. Your first sentence will be as follows:

    People have sometimes called Manhattan a forest of glass and steel.

15. Rewrite the entire passage changing all sentences from the active to the passive voice. Do not change sentence 4 or anything written on the signs. Your first sentence will be as follows:

    Manhattan is sometimes called a forest of glass and steel.

    Remember to leave out the old subject, as in the above example, unless you really need it.

Model Parents

¹Children use their parents as models, whether the models are good or bad. ²My neighbors are excellent examples.

³Mrs. Goodhouse is a conscientious housekeeper. ⁴After she went to work yesterday, her children cleaned the apartment. ⁵The eldest daughter took all the rugs outside and shook them. ⁶The middle daughter did all the dishes, and the youngest daughter vacuumed. ⁷The only boy in the family dusted and polished the furniture. ⁸When the children finished their work, they put fresh flowers in a vase for their mother.

⁹Mrs. Frowze is a terrible housekeeper. ¹⁰After she went to work yesterday, her children made a big mess. ¹¹One of them drank a soft drink and broke the bottle. ¹²The glass wasn't swept up, and the stain ruined the rug. ¹³The usual pile of garbage in the kitchen grew larger because the children ate bananas and oranges and threw the peels on the floor. ¹⁴One child drew pictures on the wall and rode his bicycle through the crayons on the floor.

¹⁵Both mothers came home to a reflection of themselves and their habits, but only *one* of them was pleased!

Steps

6. Rewrite the entire passage in the future tense using <u>will</u> at least once in every sentence. Do not change the first paragraph or sentences 3 and 9. Your second paragraph will begin as follows:

    Mrs. Goodhouse is a conscientious housekeeper. After she goes to work tomorrow, her children will clean the apartment.

9. Rewrite the entire passage in the form that uses <u>had</u> in front of every main verb. Do not change the first paragraph. Your second and third paragraphs will begin as follows:

    Mrs. Goodhouse is a conscientious housekeeper. After she came home from work yesterday, she saw that her children had cleaned the apartment.

    Mrs. Frowze is a terrible housekeeper. After she came home from work yesterday, she saw that her children had made a big mess.

Nature Abused

^{1}Our beautiful country is being destroyed by you and me. ^{2}If we are not stopped by new and stricter laws, the destruction could be completed in a few short years.

^{3}Our problem has been stated again and again by the Sierra Club, the Wilderness Club, and other environmental groups. ^{4}We have been lulled to sleep by the false image of endless resources. ^{5}Our natural environment has been taken for granted. ^{6}This kind of ignorance has been displayed even by some of our so-called leaders. ^{7}The following statement was made by one of them: "If you've seen one redwood, you've seen them all."

^{8}Strong antipollution and conservation laws must be passed by Congress. ^{9}Such laws must be enforced by federal, state, and local governments. ^{10}Finally our personal, individual concern has to be shown. ^{11}If it isn't expressed soon in day-to-day actions, we will be surrounded by, and buried in, our own garbage and wasted earth.

Steps

1. Copy the entire passage.

16. Rewrite the entire passage in the active voice. Look for the word <u>by</u> to find the new subject for each sentence or part of a sentence that you change. If you do not find the word <u>by</u>, consider what word would be a logical new subject. Your first sentence will be as follows:

    You and I are destroying our beautiful country.

    Note: Step 16 is the *reverse* of Step 15.

New York Is More

¹Many people say that New York City has the world's biggest, tallest, most, and best of everything.   ²Whether you agree or disagree, you must admit that it is a remarkable collection of people, buildings, and activities.

³First of all, New York has two of the tallest buildings in the world, the twin towers of the World Trade Center.   ⁴Each of them is 110 stories high.   ⁵Radio City Music Hall seats 6,200 people.   ⁶It is certainly the world's largest movie theater.

⁷As a center of commerce and industry, New York has no equal.   ⁸There is an unending flow of goods into and out of the city.   ⁹Wall Street is the financial capital of the world.   ¹⁰It is the home of the stock exchange and many large banks.

¹¹Fifth Avenue boasts an elegant array of clothing and jewelry stores. ¹²Some customers get bills of $50,000 or more!

¹³New York also has a huge population.   ¹⁴There are more than seven million people in its rather small area.   ¹⁵Even if New York does not have the biggest and best of everything, it seems to have the <u>most</u> of everything crowded into one place!

Steps

2. Rewrite the entire passage changing the words <u>remarkable</u> to <u>incredible</u> (sentence 2), <u>center</u> to <u>hub</u> (sentence 7), <u>unending</u> to <u>constant</u> (sentence 8), <u>elegant</u> to <u>fashionable</u> (sentence 11), <u>huge</u> to <u>enormous</u> (sentence 13), and <u>more than</u> to <u>over</u> (sentence 14).

24. Rewrite the entire passage combining sentences 3 and 4, sentences 5 and 6, sentences 9 and 10, and sentences 11 and 12 using words like <u>which</u>, <u>that</u>, and <u>who</u>. Remember that sometimes you must put one sentence *inside* the other to make the new sentence sound correct.

Old Bones

[1]Recently a crew of diggers uncovered some old bones. [2]They gave them to Michael Brinks, a teacher in the elementary school in that town. [3]Brinks was curious about the age of the bones. [4]He decided to send them to the University of Oregon for examination.

[5]Before he mailed the bones, he took them to school and showed them to his class of fifth graders. [6]He asked them how old they thought the bones were. [7]The children thought the bones came from an Ice Age horse. [8]Their teacher disagreed. [9]He didn't believe they were that old.

[10]Several weeks later, Brinks received a package that looked very official from the University of Oregon. [11]He opened it immediately. [12]He found the bones and a letter inside. [13]The letter said, "The bones in this package come from an ancient horse species which probably lived during the Ice Age."

Steps

6. Pretend that you are a fortuneteller. Rewrite the entire passage in the future tense using <u>will</u> at least once in every sentence. Your first sentence will be as follows:

   Next month a crew of diggers will uncover some old bones.

   Do *not* change the words in quotation marks in sentence 13.

15. Rewrite the entire passage in the passive voice. Do not change sentences 3, 8, and 13. Your first sentence will be as follows:

    Recently some old bones were uncovered by a crew of diggers.

20. Rewrite the entire passage replacing the underlined phrases and clauses with one or two words, or hyphenated words placed in front of the noun that the phrase or clause originally followed: <u>of diggers</u> (sentence 1), <u>in the elementary school</u> (sentence 2), <u>of fifth graders</u> (sentence 5), <u>that looked very official</u> (sentence 10), and <u>in this package</u> (sentence 13).

Old Is Beautiful

¹When I walk down Third Avenue, I love to peer into the windows of the little shops that sell old and beautiful things. ²Since I often take my walks after closing time, I cup my hands against the windows to get a small look at the treasures inside. ³I see things that tell a story without words, bits of history, often something that is clearly one of a kind. ⁴Some things look as if they have not been cared for deeply in a long time, but I know their beauty is still there beneath their worn surface.

⁵This is how I feel about old people, too. ⁶I know their value, and it hurts me when others miss it. ⁷I was raised by my grandmother and given a deep sense of the value of experience. ⁸My sister and I were taught to respect all people, regardless of their age, color, or creed. ⁹My grandmother was loved by all the people around her because she was known to be a wise and kind woman, able to do things well even in her last years.

¹⁰Old people should be treated like fine gold. ¹¹They may be tarnished by age, but they can be polished with respect. ¹²You might be surprised by their bright and shining qualities.

Steps

2. Rewrite the entire passage changing the words <u>story</u> to <u>tale</u> (sentence 3), <u>worn</u> to <u>old</u> (sentence 4), <u>deep</u> to <u>abiding</u> (sentence 7), <u>wise</u> to <u>knowing</u> (sentence 9), and <u>kind</u> to <u>affectionate</u> (sentence 9).

16. Rewrite the entire passage changing sentences 7, 8, 9, 10, and 12 to the active voice. Be sure to find a new subject for each sentence or part of a sentence that you change.

22. Rewrite the entire passage condensing the sentences indicated below by replacing several words in each with *one* of the given word forms.

sentence 1: antique/antiques	sentence 4: cherish/cherished
sentence 2: glimpse/glimpsing	sentence 9: competent/competence
sentence 3: unique/uniqueness	sentence 12: luster/lustrous

   Sentence 1 can be written correctly in two ways; however, the first example is shorter and more concise than the second:

   > When I walk down Third Avenue, I love to peer into the windows of the little antique shops.

   or

   > When I walk down Third Avenue, I love to peer into the windows of the little shops that sell antiques.

One Thing I Like

¹Last semester I asked my students in a class for basic writers to say one thing they liked about their writing. ²These are some of the responses they gave spontaneously.

Mr. R: ³I like the fact that my writing is a mirror of my thoughts. ⁴I can't lie when I write.

Ms. B: ⁵Sometimes I can think of a few ideas with real meaning. ⁶I like that.

Mr. S: ⁷Why are we talking about this?

Ms. A: ⁸I think I know. ⁹Some of us have never seen one good thing in our writing. ¹⁰It won't do any good to get praise for it if we see it as the flattery of an anxious teacher. ¹¹We have to see something good in it.

¹²I then asked some students whose silence was rather noticeable to say one thing. ¹³Mr. D. spoke with a tone of resentment in his voice.

Mr. D: ¹⁴I feel the same way as Mr. R. ¹⁵I can't lie in writing.

Ms. M: ¹⁶Do you like that fact or dislike it? ¹⁷If you like it, your writing will be better. ¹⁸Give yourself a chance!

Steps

12. Rewrite the entire passage in four paragraphs of reported speech. The second paragraph will begin as follows:

    Mr. R. said that he liked the fact that his writing was a mirror of his thoughts.

13. Rewrite the entire passage changing each portion of dialog into a separate paragraph of direct speech. The second paragraph will be as follows:

    Mr. R. said, "I like the fact that my writing is a mirror of my thoughts. I can't lie when I write."

20. Rewrite the entire passage replacing each underlined phrase and clause with one or two words, or hyphenated words placed in front of the noun that the phrase or clause originally followed: for basic writers (sentence 1), they gave spontaneously (sentence 2), with real meaning (sentence 5), of an anxious teacher (sentence 10), whose silence was rather noticeable (sentence 12), and of resentment (sentence 13).

    Remember that you must find a *new form* for the key word(s) in your original phrase or clause. Sometimes the new form may need an -'s or -s', or an -ly. Often you will end up with two words.

Politics and Fashions

[1]According to a popular theory, politics always influences fashions. [2]Right now we can see an example of the conservative trend. [3]Designers lower hems. [4]They also bring in padded shoulders and other artificial extras. [5]Women put sticky stuff on their hair, and men keep cutting their hair shorter and shorter until they end up with crewcuts. [6]We don't see many beards except on foreigners, perhaps, and older men. [7]Women increase their use of makeup.

[8]"Wait," you say. [9]"How is all this related to politics?" [10]Recent history provides an answer. [11]Can you compare the forties and fifties with the eighties? [12]Political observers see a lot of similarities. [13]They see great difference between the sixties and the eighties. [14]Maybe nobody misses the miniskirts, long hair, beards, and seemingly careless dress of the sixties, but many people miss the social consciousness of that time. [15]People are improving their appearances, but are they doing anything about their politics?

Steps

1. Copy the entire passage.

6. Rewrite the entire passage in the future tense using <u>will</u>. Do not change sentences 9–13. Your first two sentences will be as follows:

    According to a popular theory, politics will always influence fashions. In the future, we will see an example of the conservative trend.

15. Rewrite the entire passage *except* sentences 5 and 6, in the passive voice. Your first sentence will be as follows:

    According to a popular theory, fashions are always influenced by politics.

    Note: To avoid using <u>Their</u>, begin sentences 7 and 15 with the words <u>Women's</u> and <u>People's</u>.

Professor Frazier's Class

¹Everybody wants to be in Professor Frazier's class. ²Many of the upperclassmen sign up for his sections because of his widespread reputation. ³He treats all students fairly, and they can always count on his help and encouragement.

⁴Both class and small group discussions take place in Professor Frazier's class. ⁵He believes in students talking to one another in groups. ⁶All the discussions have a definite relation to students' interests. ⁷Even the issues that cause argument—race, politics, morality—are brought up because he considers it useful to meet difficult topics openly and honestly.

⁸Clearly, Professor Frazier has all the necessary features of a good teacher. ⁹Since he inspires his students, they often become deeply involved in their studies.

Steps

17. Imagine the Professor Frazier is a terrible teacher, not an excellent one. Rewrite the entire passage making each affirmative sentence negative so that your composition states just the opposite of what the model passage says. In some sentences, you can change the meaning by simply adding the word not. In others, you will need other negative words like no, none, nothing, nobody, never, neither, and nor. Your first sentence will be as follows:

    Nobody wants to be in Professor Frazier's class.

    Note: Not every verb in the passage needs to be negative. At least one negative should be used in each sentence, but a few things in the passage as a whole remain affirmative.

22. Rewrite the entire passage condensing the indicated sentences below by replacing several words in each with *one* of the given word forms.

    sentence 5: interact/interaction   sentence 7: confront/confrontation
    sentence 6: relevant/relevancy   sentence 8: essential/essentials
    sentence 7: controversial/   sentence 9: invest/invested
            controversy

Rich and Poor

[1]In the late 1970s, a steady decrease in the number of poor Americans marked the so-called war on poverty. [2]Most people saw this decrease as a natural result of our prosperity and expected it to go on indefinitely. [3]In 1979, however, newspapers noted a disturbing *increase* in the number of poor Americans. [4]Nothing stopped the reversal. [5]How did we lose this war without a real fight?

[6]First, people lost more skilled jobs. [7]Big companies moved factories to Mexico, South Korea, and Taiwan. [8]Often employment agencies could offer skilled workers only unskilled jobs. [9]The situation forced steel workers to become security guards. [10]Obviously, their income dropped dramatically.

[11]Second, government gave people less help. [12]It cut back most social programs. [13]It put education and health care farther and farther below military spending. [14]At the same time, it increased taxes.

[15]Still, these changes do not affect all Americans equally. [16]A major journal of American business publishes an interesting list of the 400 richest people in the country. [17]In a recent year, that list included a number of billionaires. [18]The following year, the number doubled!

Steps

2. Rewrite the entire passage changing the words steady to regular (sentence 1), natural to inevitable (sentence 2), go on to continue (sentence 2), disturbing to unfortunate (sentence 3), unskilled to service (sentence 8), dramatically to significantly (sentence 10), and interesting to useful (sentence 16).

10. Rewrite the entire passage changing every sentence except 1, 2, 17, and 18 to the form that uses have or has in front of every main verb. Sentence 3 will be as follows:

    Since 1979, however, newspapers have noted a disturbing *increase* in the number of poor Americans.

15. Rewrite the entire passage changing all sentences from the active to the passive voice. Your first sentence will be as follows:

    In the late 1970s, the so-called war on poverty was marked by a steady decrease in the number of poor Americans.

    Note: Rewrite the two negative sentences 4 and 15 in as natural a way as possible.

40

Rock Rebirth

¹In the mid-eighties, rock music came alive again. ²When Michael Jackson made his *Thriller* album in 1983, even old people in their forties went out and bought it. ³The music video business arose almost entirely out of the album's hit single "Beat It." ⁴Teenagers began coming home from school and turning on MTV (music television). ⁵Although discos did not disappear altogether, their focus changed from a showy floor to a large screen on which the latest music videos could be shown.

⁶The music itself changed, too. ⁷Some of it got sharper, some of it got sweeter, but the beat developed in a lot of different directions. ⁸That insistent, and eventually boring, disco beat gave way to an extensive variety of rhythms.

⁹One of the high points of the rock rebirth was a major event of 1985: the recording of "We Are the World" by an ensemble of about 50 rock stars, young and old, black and white, to help starving people in Africa. ¹⁰They showed that rock was alive and well, and its heart was beating for more than fun and money.

Steps

2. Rewrite the entire passage changing the words turning on to watching (sentence 4), showy to elaborate (sentence 5), large to huge (sentence 5), a lot of to lots of (sentence 7), extensive to wide (sentence 8), major to important (sentence 9), and ensemble to group (sentence 9).

6. Pretend that you are writing this story in the seventies, and it is a prediction about the future. Rewrite the entire passage in the future tense using the word will at least once in every sentence. Your first sentence will be as follows:

   In the mid-eighties, rock music will come alive again.

9. Rewrite the entire passage in the form that uses had in front of every main verb. Do not change sentence 2, the end of sentence 5, or sentence 10. Your first sentence will be as follows:

   In the mid-eighties, rock music had come alive again.

Rush Hour Blues

[1]Why does the commuter frequently look so miserable?   [2]Here is the sad story of one railroad commuter.   [3]He is a victim of the rush hour blues.

[4]He gets up at 6:00 A.M. and eats a quick breakfast.   [5]Then he drives himself to the train station.   [6]He arrives on time, but his train doesn't. [7]When it finally comes, he squeezes on and finds there are no more seats. [8]He has to stand with his briefcase between his knees.   [9]There is simply no room to put it down.   [10]Suddenly, a gust of cold air hits him in the face. [11]The window is broken!   [12]He remembers the previous summer.   [13]At that time, the windows didn't even open.

[14]The conductor makes his way through the crowd and asks for tickets. [15]The commuter looks for his ticket.   [16]He drops everything clumsily in the search.   [17]The conductor grumbles impatiently.

[18]Finally the train reaches its destination.   [19]The commuter is already exhausted.   [20]He says to himself, "What a way to start the day!"

Steps

4.   Rewrite the entire passage changing the word commuter to commuters wherever it appears. You will be writing about many commuters, but only one train and one conductor. Your first three sentences will be as follows:

Why do commuters frequently look so miserable? Here is the sad story of railroad commuters. They are victims of the rush hour blues.

7.   Pretend that the story above actually happened to one commuter. Rewrite the entire passage changing everything except the first paragraph to the past tense. The first sentence in your second paragraph will be as follows:

He got up at 6:00 A.M. and ate a quick breakfast.

26.   Rewrite the entire passage. Combine sentences 2 and 3, sentences 4 and 5, sentences 8 and 9, sentences 12 and 13, sentences 15 and 16, and sentences 18 and 19 in the *shortest and clearest way possible.* Don't leave out any of the information.

The Schoolyard

¹Whoever said that childhood is simple and happy?   ²If you watch children playing after school, you begin to get some idea of their feelings.

³In one corner of the schoolyard, two teams play basketball.   ⁴One player leaps to the hoop and smashes the ball through it.   ⁵His teammates cheer him on.   ⁶Meanwhile, a boy all alone watches the action with close attention. ⁷His body is completely still, but his eyes follow every movement of the players.   ⁸Obviously, he longs to join them, but he is being ignored completely.

⁹In another corner, some girls stand in a tight little circle around one girl.   ¹⁰She imitates a teacher who passes by while leaving school.   ¹¹Her friends giggle, and she makes the most of the attention she gets.   ¹²Two other girls watch nearby.   ¹³They make a face in disapproval of her behavior.

¹⁴Only the surface shows.   ¹⁵Somewhere deeper, thoughts race, feelings are hurt, friendships are tested.   ¹⁶Some children learn more in the schoolyard than in school.

Steps

8.   Pretend that everything described in the passage is going on at this very moment. Rewrite the entire passage in the tense that uses a form of BE in front of every main verb and –ing at the end of it. Use at least one –ing form in every sentence except the first part of sentence 7. Your second paragraph will begin as follows:

> In one corner of the schoolyard, two teams are playing basketball.

21.   Rewrite the entire passage using the words below to replace *two or more words* in the indicated sentences.

sentence 2: sense   sentence 9: huddle
sentence 6: intently   sentence 10: departing
sentence 7: immobile   sentence 13: frown

Remember to add a small word if necessary to make the new word fit in correctly.

43

Scorpions

[1]Scorpions are people who were born under the zodiac sign of the Scorpion (October 23 to November 21).   [2]Their main characteristic is intensity—like the sting of a scorpion.   [3]They are represented by artists of great fame such as Bizet, Picasso, Dostoyevsky, Keats, and Turgenev.

[4]Scorpions have both strong virtues and strong vices.   [5]On the positive side, they are very serious and energetic people.   [6]They are usually very successful in their life's work.   [7]They show their outstanding abilities as artists and scientists.   [8]On the negative side, they must guard against touchiness and cruelty.   [9]Also, they have a tendency to make fun of things. [10]They treat love seriously.   [11]However, their intense love can easily turn to jealousy or hate if the loved one gives them any reason for it.

[12]Fortunately, Scorpions' ability to control themselves is unusually strong.   [13]They can handle their powerful feelings.   [14]They hardly ever lose their composure completely.

Steps

5. Rewrite the entire passage changing the word <u>Scorpions</u> to <u>a Scorpion</u> wherever it appears. Refer to that person as "he" or "she," but not both. Your first sentence will be as follows:

   A Scorpion is a person who was born under the zodiac sign of the Scorpion (October 23 to November 21).

21. Rewrite the entire passage using words below to replace *two or more words* in the indicated sentences.

sentence 3: renowned	sentence 11: provokes
sentence 7: excel	sentence 12: self-control
sentence 9: mock	sentence 14: seldom

    Sentence 3 will look like this after it has been condensed:

    They are represented by renowned artists such as Bizet, Picasso, Dostoyevsky, Keats, and Turgenev.

23. Rewrite the entire passage combining sentences 6 and 7, sentences 8 and 9, sentences 10 and 11, and sentences 13 and 14 with the word <u>and</u>, <u>but</u>, or <u>so</u>. Leave out the word <u>Also</u> in sentence 9 and the word <u>However</u> in sentence 11. Make your new sentences as short and clear as possible.

Six Cats

[1]Elliot was 45 years old, unmarried, and miserable. [2]He was living with his mother and her six cats in a small apartment. [3]Although he liked his mother, he hated her cats. [4]They slept in his bed and made him sneeze terribly.

[5]One day Elliot met Evelyn, a reference librarian, and everything changed.

Elliot: [6]Evelyn, I love you, and I want to marry you very soon.

Evelyn: [7]That sounds wonderful.

Elliot: [8]There are a few things I have to know first, however.

Evelyn: [9]Ask me anything, dear.

Elliot: [10]Have you been looking for a man like me?

Evelyn: [11]Yes, and I'm sure I've found him.

Elliot: [12]What will you do if I lose all my hair tomorrow?

Evelyn: [13]I'll still love you. You can count on that.

Elliot: [14]Do you have any questions for me?

Evelyn: [15]No, but I hope you love cats as much as you love me. [16]My six cats are afraid to sleep alone, so they always sleep with me.

Steps

12. Rewrite the entire passage in three paragraphs using reported speech. You will have to rewrite all the dialog as one paragraph. Your third paragraph will begin as follows:

    Elliot told Evelyn that he loved her and wanted to marry her very soon.

13. Rewrite the entire passage changing each portion of dialog into a separate paragraph of direct speech. You will need to add quotation marks, commas, and phrases such as Elliot said to your composition. Your third paragraph will begin as follows:

    Elliot said, "Evelyn, I love you, and I want to marry you very soon."

Spendthrifts

[1]I have never been able to make sense of my attitude toward money. [2]I can walk into a department store and spend $700 on a suit, then go home and squeeze three cups of tea out of a single teabag! [3]Am I a spendthrift, a miser, or both?

[4]A spendthrift is a person who likes to spend money. [5]She always buys things without regard to cost. [6]All her spending gives her pleasure, so she indulges herself with shopping sprees. [7]She is both warmhearted and generous. [8]She has a lot of friends because she often treats everybody to drinks and meals. [9]She would even give or lend money to her worst enemy! [10]Some people can accept a spendthrift's habits very easily. [11]They consider such a person immature, but they enjoy being with her, nevertheless.

[12]Are you a little like the person just described? [13]If you are one of the big spenders of the world, you will always have debts, but you may have a lot of fun, too.

Steps

3. Pretend that the spendthrift in this passage is a man instead of a woman. Rewrite the entire passage making the necessary changes in the second paragraph only. The first two sentences of your second paragraph will be as follows:

   A spendthrift is a person who likes to spend money. He always buys things without regard to cost.

4. Rewrite the entire passage changing the words a spendthrift to spendthrifts in the second paragraph only. You will be writing about many spendthrifts instead of just one. Be careful with the word spendthrift's in sentence 10! The first sentence of your second paragraph will be as follows:

   Spendthrifts are people who like to spend money.

17. Rewrite the entire passage changing the words a spendthrift to a miser in the second paragraph only and the words worst enemy to best friend. Then change all the sentences in the second and third paragraphs from the affirmative to the negative so that your composition describes a person just the opposite of a spendthrift. The first sentence of your second paragraph will be as follows:

   A miser is a person who does not (doesn't) like to spend money.

   Remember to use different negative words like no, not, never, and none and not to change every single verb.

A Thanksgiving Celebration

¹Dick Barnett is a man who loves to cook. ²Every year on Thanksgiving, he gets up at 6:00 A.M. to prepare for his family celebration. ³He vacuums the floor, dusts the furniture, and puts away unnecessary things. ⁴He takes his turkey out of the refrigerator at about 10:00 A.M. and makes a delicious stuffing to put inside it. ⁵He sets the oven at 400°, and when it's preheated, he puts the turkey in and turns the temperature down to 325°. ⁶Then he prepares all the vegetables. ⁷He usually bakes bread the day before because he doesn't have time to do everything on Thanksgiving Day.

⁸His family arrives between 2:00 and 3:00 P.M. ⁹His sister-in-law always brings apple cider and a pie. ¹⁰His niece sets the table, and his nephew carves the turkey. ¹¹Then all of them sit down to eat. ¹²And how they love to eat!

¹³After the main part of the meal, the whole family takes a walk before they can eat dessert. ¹⁴Dick gives his family most of the leftovers because he doesn't trust himself with so much food in the house.

Steps

3. Rewrite the entire passage changing the name <u>Dick Barnett</u> to <u>Sally Barnett</u>. You will be writing about a woman instead of a man, and you should continue writing about a woman throughout the composition. Your first sentence will be as follows:

    Sally Barnett is a woman who loves to cook.

4. Rewrite the entire passage changing the name <u>Dick Barnett</u> to <u>Dick and Judy Barnett</u>. You will be writing about a couple instead of one man, and you should continue writing about a couple throughout the composition. Your first sentence will be as follows:

    Dick and Judy Barnett are people who love to cook.

    Note: Because this step involves singular and plural, it has more than 30 changes in it. Imagine that Dick and Judy work as a close team. When you finish your composition, proofread it very carefully to see that it sounds right.

7. Pretend that you are remembering Dick Barnett and his previous Thanksgiving celebrations. Rewrite the entire passage in the past tense. Your first sentence will be as follows:

    Dick Barnett was a man who loved to cook.

The Throwaway Society

¹In his book <u>Future Shock</u>, author Alvin Toffler writes that America has become a throwaway society. ²Cardboard milk containers and rockets are only two examples. ³Such products are created for short-term or one-time use. ⁴They are becoming more numerous and more important to modern living. ⁵Toffler thinks that man's relationship with things will grow increasingly temporary.

⁶As proof of this trend, Toffler cites such products as disposable diapers, paper napkins and tissues, and nonreturnable bottles. ⁷Vegetables are encased in plastic bags. ⁸The bags can be dropped into a pot of boiling water and thrown away after cooking. ⁹TV dinners are heated in throwaway trays. ¹⁰They are even served in them. ¹¹All these things are quickly used up. ¹²Then they are ruthlessly eliminated. ¹³In Toffler's view, the American home has become little more than a large processing plant.

¹⁴Toffler further believes that his countrymen are developing throwaway values to match their throwaway products. ¹⁵He says that easy disposability leads to shorter man-thing relationships. ¹⁶People were once linked to a few objects for a long time. ¹⁷Now they are linked to many objects briefly.

Steps

11. The book <u>Future Shock</u> was published some time ago. Rewrite the entire passage using the past tense. Begin with the following sentence:

    In his book <u>Future Shock</u>, author Alvin Toffler wrote that America had become a throwaway society.

14. Rewrite the entire passage changing all reported speech to direct speech. Determine which are the writer's exact words and put quotation marks around them. Your first sentence will be as follows:

    In his book <u>Future Shock</u>, author Alvin Toffler writes, "America has become a throwaway society."

    Note: You will have to start a new quotation in each of the three paragraphs.

26. Rewrite the entire passage. Combine sentences 2, 3, and 4, sentences 7 and 8, sentences 9 and 10, sentences 11 and 12, and sentences 16 and 17 in the shortest and clearest way possible. Do not change the meaning of the passage in any way.

Visitors

[1]Every year millions of people visit the United States. [2]Most of them fly into big city airports, but some of them arrive by ship. [3]No matter how they travel, they are bound to meet surprises.

[4]Most visitors are amazed at all the contrasts, especially in the major cities. [5]For example, they see and hear people walking fast, talking fast, and eating fast. Yet it seems to take forever to get through downtown traffic on public transportation. [6]Visitors are fascinated by the height of city skyscrapers with their clean lines of glass and steel. [7]But, looking down, they find streets that are dirty and cluttered, always undergoing some kind of construction or repair. [8]If the visitors do not speak English, they have a hard time making themselves understood. [9]They miss the multilingual signs and employees found in many other foreign cities. [10]However, at the same time, they hear more languages around them than they might hear anywhere else.

[11]What impression do these visitors take home? [12]Maybe they say to their friends, "This time I visited one city; next time I'll visit the rest of the U.S.!"

Steps

1. Copy the entire passage.

5. Rewrite the entire passage changing the words <u>Most visitors</u> to <u>The average visitor</u> in sentence 4. This means that you will be writing about one person instead of many people throughout the rest of the composition. Your second paragraph will begin as follows:

   The average visitor is amazed at all the contrasts, especially in the major cities.

7. Rewrite the entire passage changing the words <u>Every year</u> to <u>Last year</u> in sentence 1. You will be writing in the past tense throughout your composition. Your first sentence will be as follows:

   Last year millions of people visited the United States.

   Note: Do not change any of the words in the quotation in sentence 12.

Wheels

[1]Americans have a passion for anything on wheels.　[2]A person spends a good part of his infancy in carriages and strollers.　[3]Later he can have his first self-propelled wheels in the form of roller skates, a bicycle, or a skateboard. [4]As an adult, his choice of wheels is wide and still growing.

[5]Mopeds are a familiar sight on city and suburban streets.　[6]They are basically motorized bicycles.　[7]According to consumer magazines, they have both advantages and disadvantages.　[8]They score high on operating costs and fuel conservation.　[9]They get 100 miles to a gallon of gas.　[10]Furthermore, they are easy to park.　[11]Some states still do not require moped owners to have insurance or protection such as helmets.　[12]This situation is convenient for owners but also dangerous.　[13]Mopeds travel at only 20 to 30 miles per hour.　[14]This speed is enough to cause serious injury in an accident.

[15]Some people say mopeds are the perfect compromise between a bicycle and a motorcycle.　[16]Others feel they run a poor second to either one. [17]Happy sales representatives say,　[18]"Just look at the figures.　[19]You'll see a lot more people like them than dislike them.　[20]They're selling like crazy!"

Steps

1. Copy the entire passage.

5. Rewrite the entire passage changing the word <u>mopeds</u> to <u>the moped</u> wherever it appears. You will be writing about one typical moped instead of all mopeds. The first two sentences of your second paragraph will be as follows:

   The moped is the newest thing on city and suburban streets. It is basically a motorized bicycle.

25. Rewrite the entire passage using words like <u>if</u>, <u>while</u>, and <u>because</u> or <u>which</u>, <u>who</u>, and <u>whose</u> to combine six out of seven of the following pairs of sentences: sentences 2 and 3, sentences 5 and 6, sentences 8 and 9, sentences 11 and 12, sentences 13 and 14, sentences 15 and 16, and sentences 18 and 19. Leave out the word <u>Later</u> in sentence 3 if you combine sentences 2 and 3.

Who's Tom Cruise?

¹Recently I asked some of my older friends what they thought of Tom Cruise. ²Some of them looked as if they wondered why I was asking, and others really seemed not to know whom I was talking about. ³These were some of the responses:

Mr. A: ⁴Who's he?

Ms. B: ⁵I've never heard of him. ⁶Is he the one that was in <u>Platoon</u>?

⁷I told my friends that I was talking about one of the most promising young men in Hollywood, and I mentioned some of his TV and film credits.

Ms. C: ⁸I know who you mean! ⁹He's that good-looking guy everyone's crazy about these days.

Mr. D: ¹⁰Do you really think he's good looking? ¹¹He acts as if he's in love with himself.

Dr. E: ¹²I would, too, if I looked like him.

Ms. F: ¹³I promise I won't tell anyone that you all are a little bit envious of a Hollywood star.

Steps

4. Rewrite the entire passage, including the title, adding the words <u>and Don Johnson</u> to the end of the first sentence. You will be writing about two movie and TV stars instead of just one throughout your composition. Your first sentence will be as follows:

   Recently I asked some of my older friends what they thought of Tom Cruise and Don Johnson.

12. Rewrite the entire passage in four paragraphs of reported speech. You will have to rewrite the first two people's remarks as one paragraph and the last four as one paragraph as well. Your second paragraph will begin as follows:

    Mr. A. asked who he was.

13. Rewrite the entire passage changing each remark into a separate paragraph of direct speech. You will have to add quotation marks, commas, and phrases such as <u>Mr. A. asked</u>. Your second paragraph will be as follows:

    Mr. A. asked, "Who's he?"

Writing Well

¹In his book <u>What Do I Do Monday?</u>, John Holt talks about problems college students are having with writing.   ²He says that in order to write well, young people will have to learn how to talk long and seriously to a friend they can trust.   ³If they are able to express themselves through speaking, they will also become writers with a good deal of fluency.

⁴Holt says that teachers can encourage good writing by setting up classrooms where conversations among friends will take place.   ⁵In Holt's view, there are unfortunately very few writing classrooms with such encouragement.   ⁶In fact, many teachers give the impression that talking and writing are for manipulating others.   ⁷Holt thinks that is why so many students in the universities believe that it is not possible to use words honestly.   ⁸Instead, they feel nearly all speaking and writing involves lying.   ⁹Therefore, many students have become suspicious of words in print—and sometimes words in general.

Steps

11.   Rewrite the entire passage in the past tense. Your first sentence will be as follows:

> In his book <u>What Do I Do Monday?</u>, John Holt talked about problems college students were having with writing.

14.   Rewrite the entire passage changing all reported speech to direct speech. Decide what Holt's exact words were and put quotation marks around them. Your first two sentences will be as follows:

> In his book <u>What Do I Do Monday?</u>, John Holt talks about problems college students are having with writing. He says, "In order to write well, young people will have to learn how to talk long and seriously to a friend they can trust.

19.   Underline the following phrases and clauses: <u>they can trust</u> (sentence 2), <u>with a good deal of fluency</u> (sentence 3), <u>among friends</u> (sentence 4), <u>with such encouragement</u> (sentence 5), <u>in the universities</u> (sentence 7), and <u>in print</u> (sentence 9). Then, look at each phrase or clause and decide which word or words could be used *in another form* to modify the noun that the phrase or clause originally followed. Here is an example:

> . . . a friend they can trust   a trustworthy friend
>   *or*
>   a trusted friend

Rewrite the entire passage placing the new forms of the key word(s) in the underlined phrases and clauses in front of the noun that each phrase or clause originally followed.

52

The Yenta

¹Neighborhood yentas are well-known women.   ²They spend most of their time watching people around them.   ³"Yenta" is a Yiddish word.   ⁴It means busybody or gossip.   ⁵The yentas earn this title.   ⁶Nobody on their street is safe from their eyes and tongue.

⁷Yentas certainly are not bad people.   ⁸They pass on messages and advice.   ⁹They give up-to-the-minute weather reports.   ¹⁰They know who is doing what.   ¹¹They see, hear, and know all and usually repeat it.   ¹²They have appointed themselves neighborhood reporters and guardians.

¹³Some of the yentas' neighbors accuse them of being so concerned with local affairs that they neglect their own.   ¹⁴Sometimes, however, a child has to be found, or a mugging has to be reported.   ¹⁵Then the yentas' services are invaluable.   ¹⁶Every neighborhood grudgingly appreciates its yentas.   ¹⁷It doesn't matter what their color, creed, or accent is.

Steps

5.   Rewrite the entire passage changing the word <u>yentas</u> to <u>the yenta</u> wherever it appears. You will be writing about one woman instead of many women throughout your composition. Your first sentence will be as follows:

   The neighborhood yenta is a well-known woman.

7.   Pretend that you are writing in the twenty-first century and that yentas have disappeared. Rewrite the entire passage in the past tense, but do not change sentences 3 and 4. Your first sentence will be as follows:

   Years ago, neighborhood yentas were well-known women.

26.   Rewrite the entire passage. Combine sentences 1 and 2, sentences 3 and 4, sentences 5 and 6, sentences 8, 9, and 10, sentences 14 and 15, and sentences 16 and 17 in the shortest and clearest way possible.

Zero Hour

[1]An astronaut is sitting tensely in a command module. [2]He is waiting for zero hour, the moment of lift-off. [3]Some thought of danger must be with him at this time. [4]Still, he remains calm.

[5]Long before the big moment arrives, the astronaut is put through a rigorous training program. [6]He receives instruction in all space-related subjects. [7]He also learns through simulation of space flight. [8]His body must be in excellent condition before a real flight.

[9]Three days before launching, he starts a special diet. [10]During the last 24 hours, he is isolated from his family to avoid emotional farewells. [11]The isolation also encourages maximum concentration.

[12]When zero hour is only three hours away, he takes an elevator to the top of the spaceship and enters the command module. [13]He straps himself into his seat. [14]When he has checked everything with Mission Control, there is nothing to do but wait. [15]He tries to relax. [16]If he doesn't succeed, can you blame him?

Steps

3.   Pretend that the astronaut in the passage is a woman. Rewrite the entire passage making the necessary changes. Your first two sentences will be as follows:

   An astronaut is sitting tensely in a command module. She is waiting for zero hour, the moment of lift-off.

4.   Rewrite the entire passage changing the words An astronaut to Two astronauts in sentence 1. This means that you will be writing about two men instead of one man throughout your composition. Your first sentence will be:

   Two astronauts are sitting tensely in a command module.

23.   Rewrite the entire passage combining sentences 1 and 2, sentences 3 and 4., sentences 6 and 7, sentences 10 and 11, sentences 12 and 13, and sentences 14 and 15 with the words and, but, or so. You can leave out words like still and also. Make your new sentences as short as possible without losing any information.

Student Record Sheet

No.	Date	Title of Passage	Step(s)	Errors
1				
2				
3				
4				
5				
6				
7				
8				
9				
10				
11				
12				
13				
14				
15				
16				
17				
18				
19				
20				
21				
22				
23				
24				
25				
26				
27				
28				
29				
30				
31				

continued

Student Record Sheet—*continued*

No.	Date	Title of Passage	Step(s)	Errors
32				
33				
34				
35				
36				
37				
38				
39				
40				
41				
42				
43				
44				
45				
46				
47				
48				
49				
50				
51				
52				
53				
54				
55				
56				
57				
58				
59				
60				
61				
62				

Sequence of Passages on Each Step

Step 1
a. The Light-Fingered Elephant
b. Coffee Breakthrough
c. Politics and Fashion
d. Capricornians
e. Nature Abused
f. Wheels
g. Bureaucracy
h. Visitors

Step 2
a. New York Is More
b. Late Night City
c. Detectives
d. Central Park
e. Fire and I
f. Rock Rebirth
g. Rich and Poor
h. Old Is Beautiful

Step 3
a. A Good Friend
b. Cancerians
c. Spendthrifts
d. Zero Hour
e. A Thanksgiving Celebration
f. The Light-Fingered Elephant

Step 4
a. A Thanksgiving Celebration
b. Zero Hour
c. Who's Tom Cruise?
d. Librans
e. Detectives
f. Spendthrifts
g. Rush Hour Blues
h. Changing Roles

Step 5
a. Blue Collar
b. The Yenta
c. Scorpions
d. Fire and I
e. Capricornians
f. Keep a Cat
g. Wheels
h. Visitors

Step 6
a. Rock Rebirth
b. Model Parents
c. Old Bones
d. Cancerians
e. Guest of Honor
f. Politics and Fashion

Step 7
a. Visitors
b. A Thanksgiving Celebration
c. Keep a Cat
d. Rush Hour Blues
e. The Yenta
f. Blue Collar

Step 8
a. The Schoolyard
b. Fire Alarm
c. Block Associaitons
d. Central Park
e. Late Night City
f. Antibilingualism

Step 9
a. Guest of Honor
b. Model Parents
c. Rock Rebirth

Step 10
a. Anitbilingualism
b. Block Associations
c. Fire Alarm
d. Rich and Poor
e. Manhattan Green
f. Changing Roles

Step 11
a. A Letter Home
b. Big Business
c. Writing Well
d. The Throwaway Society

Step 12
a. Six Cats
b. One Thing I Like
c. Don't Run Away
d. Who's Tom Cruise?

Step 13
a. Who's Tom Cruise?
b. Don't Run Away
c. One Thing I Like
d. Six Cats

Step 14
a. Big Business
b. The Throwaway Society
c. Writing Well
d. A Letter Home

Step 15
A. Bureaucracy
b. Manhattan Green
c. Rich and Poor
d. Old Bones
e. Politics and Fashion
f. Guest of Honor

Step 16
a. Nature Abused
b. Colleges Today
c. Leaders
d. Old Is Beautiful

Step 17	a. Professor Frazier's Class	c. Spendthrifts
	b. Give It Up	d. A Good Friend
Step 18	a. Block Associations	c. Detectives
	b. Librans	d. A Letter Home
Step 19	a. Writing Well	c. Colleges Today
	b. Cancerians	d. Big Business
Step 20	a. Keep a Cat	c. Old Bones
	b. One Thing I Like	d. Blue Collar
Step 21	a. Scorpions	c. Changing Roles
	b. A Good Friend	d. The Schoolyard
Step 22	a. Old Is Beautiful	c. Leaders
	b. Don't Run Away	d. Professor Frazier's Class
Step 23	a. Capricornians	c. Scorpions
	b. Fire Alarm	d. Zero Hour
Step 24	a. Central Park	c. Antibilingualism
	b. Leaders	d. New York Is More
Step 25	a. Fire and I	c. Librans
	b. Wheels	d. Give It Up
Step 26	a. The Throwaway Society	c. Rush Hour Blues
	b. Coffee Breakthrough	d. The Yenta